32
Zesty Pizzas

By Bev Bennett and Kim Upton

BARRON'S
Woodbury, New York • London • Toronto • Sydney

All inquiries should be addressed to:

Barron's Educational Series, Inc.
113 Crossways Park Drive
Woodbury, New York 11797

International Standard Book
No. 0-8120-5536-5
Library of Congress Catalog Card
No. 83-10013

**Library of Congress Cataloging
in Publication Data**
Bennett, Bev.
    32 zesty pizzas.

    (Barron's easy cooking series)
    Includes index.
    1. Pizza. I. Upton, Kim.
II. Title. III. Title:
Thirty-two zesty pizzas.
IV. Series.
TX770.B47 1983   641.8'24   83-10013
ISBN 0-8120-5536-5

PRINTED IN THE
UNITED STATES OF AMERICA
3 4 5 6   9 8 7 6 5 4 3 2 1

Credits

Photography
Color photographs: Matthew Klein
Food preparation: Helen Feingold
Stylist: Linda Cheverton
Sources for props: All stainless-steel flatware
    from Manhattan Ad Hoc, 843 Lexington
    Avenue, New York City; all laboratory
    glass and Cauldethon saucepan from
    Manhattan Ad Hoc; handthrown porcelain
    plates by Lynn Evans for Gordon Foster
    Antiques, 1322 Third Avenue, New York
    City; all pizza pans, accessories for pizza
    and plates used for recipes 11, 16, 18, 21,
    23, 24, 26 from Dean and DeLuca, 121
    Prince Street, New York City.

Authors Bev Bennett and Kim Upton are
    food writers for the *Chicago Sun-Times*

Cover and book design Milton Glaser, Inc.

Series editor Carole Berglie

INTRODUCTION

There's a pandemonium in the land that has even fancy food lovers celebrating a simple food baked in a pan. That food is pizza. Given its strong and steady growth in popularity, it's more than just pie in the sky.

It's great eating for modest work and money.

Where pizza was once children's food, it has finally come of age. No longer is it gummy dough topped with bland tomato sauce and a shot of cheese. Pizza is evolving into new flavor forms and even new shapes.

Pizza can be subtle and almost light, as it appears in pesto pizza with fresh mushrooms. It can be exotic, just as it is in Virginia Motan's Pakistani-style pizza with curried vegetable toppings. It can even be sweet, as is the just-for-fun (but delicious) "mock" pizza cheesecake we've created for dessert.

And it's shaping up in new ways, too. Pinwheel pizzas, pizza eggrolls, and calzone—the folded-over pizza sandwich from Italy—all illustrate this.

Here in Chicago, trendy restaurants are serving such innovative dishes as pizza with a goat cheese topping. But this is just one in a series of inventions that are being served in our town.

Just as Italy has become the adopted home of pasta (which actually came from China), Chicago has adopted pizza as one of its home-town foods. While the original idea certainly wasn't ours, we have rolled it and stretched it and filled it so that now, when thoughts turn to Chicago and food, deep-dish and stuffed (also called double-crust) pizzas come immediately to mind.

Yet even in Chicago, pizza need not be either the deep-dish or stuffed creations based on a heavy yeast crust, tomato sauce, sausage, and pounds of mozzarella cheese.

And it need not be difficult to make. In fact, this is another reason for pizza's growing popularity. The only cooking skills necessary are stirring, sautéeing, baking, and kneading.

If kneading is a mystery, think of it as exercising the dough until it becomes smooth and slightly elastic. Begin by lifting the dough end closest to you and folding it in half away from you. Press down hard when you fold it. Then turn the dough 45 degrees and repeat the process. If the dough is sticky and hard to work with, sprinkle the work surface with a little flour or lightly grease your hands with vegetable oil or butter.

Pizza requires no fancy equipment. While some of the new pizza baking items—such as stone baking surfaces—are fun, we can create wonderful pizza dishes with only a few basic tools.

Start with a cookie sheet or a thin-crust pizza pan. Both are available in baking departments of most supermarkets. For larger double-crust or deep-dish pizzas, a round 10-inch pan with 2-inch sides works well, or use a casserole dish of similar size. Even the once difficult-to-find, 14-inch deep-dish pizza pans are beginning to pop up in housewares sections of many major department stores. And while even the simple disc pizza cutter is handy, the same easy slicing can be done with a sharp knife or a pair of scissors. Other than that, all that is needed is a couple of bowls, measuring tools, and a few saucepans. And your imagination.

Pizza isn't attractive simply because it's easy, delicious, and has a pretty face. Baked pizza freezes well, making it a convenient food for people in a hurry.

To freeze leftover pizza, wrap it tightly in moisture-proof material. Most pizzas can be frozen except those with an egg/quiche filling and those that rely on crisp vegetables for flavor and character. To reheat, cover loosely with foil and place on a preheated cookie sheet in a preheated 350-degree oven until cheese is bubbling. Cooking time will vary with pizza size and thickness, but a four-inch-wide slice of deep-dish pizza, for example, defrosts and cooks in about 40 minutes.

Baked pizza crust, tomato pizza sauce, and grated cheese also freeze well separately for purposes of pizza creation. Wrap crust in moisture-proof material. Pour tomato pizza sauce and grated cheese into separate plastic freezer containers. All 3 will keep for up to 6 months in the freezer.

To defrost baked crust, preheat an empty pizza pan in a 400-degree oven for 10 minutes. Place frozen pizza crust on pan and cover loosely with foil. Bake for 10 minutes or until center of crust is warm; the baking time will vary with thickness of crust.

To defrost tomato pizza sauce, place in small saucepan, cover, and cook over low heat, stirring occasionally, for about 15 minutes; the cooking time will vary with amount of pizza sauce.

Frozen, grated cheese doesn't require thawing; use it as it comes from the freezer.

To rewarm cold pizza, cover loosely with foil and place in a 350-degree oven for 20 minutes or until pizza is heated through; the re-heating time will vary with size and thickness of pizza.

Pizza is so easy to make that it requires only these few hints to create it successfully. Remember:

● to double-check the expiration date on yeast to make sure it is still active.

● all-purpose flour should be used unless otherwise specified.

● that yeast dough rises better in a warm place.

● that 1 pound of cheese equals about 4 cups of grated cheese; that 1 medium green pepper is about 1 cup chopped; that 1 medium onion is about 1 cup chopped, and that 6 or 7 large mushrooms make 1 cup when sliced.

● that prebaking the pizza crust will keep it from becoming soggy. Pricking the dough first will prevent air bubbles.

● to sauté garlic over low heat only until it becomes soft. If allowed to turn brown or black, garlic becomes bitter.

● that garlic powder can be substituted for garlic in most recipes (1 garlic clove equals about 1 teaspoon garlic powder) but it will not taste as good.

● that traditional pizza ingredients can be used in foods other than pizza. For a pizza omelet, prepare your favorite omelet recipe. When omelet is almost done, top with ½ cup tomato pizza sauce, any combination of green peppers, mushrooms, onions or anchovies, and sprinkle generously with mozzarella cheese. Place under the broiler until the cheese melts.

● that when summer's ripened-on-the-vine tomatoes aren't available, forego the fresh tomato pizza sauce and prepare the quick tomato pizza sauce instead. The flavor will be better.

● that pizza is appropriate for breakfast. To make a breakfast pizza, butter 2 English muffin halves. Top each half with a tomato slice, then a slice of

...ozzarella cheese. Bake in a 400-degree oven until
...he cheese gets bubbly, about 5 minutes.

...although pizza preparation times from start to
...nish seem long, you will spend only a portion of
...hat in the kitchen working.

...to use good pizza recipes like those in this
...ook.

UNDERSTANDING THE
RECIPE ANALYSES

...or each recipe in this book, you'll note that we
...ave provided data on the quantities of protein,
...t, sodium, carbohydrates, and potassium, as well
...s the number of calories (kcal) per serving. If you
...re on a low-calorie diet or are watching your in-
...ke of sodium, for example, these figures should
...elp you gauge your eating habits and help you
...alance your meals. Bear in mind, however, that
...he calculations are fundamentally estimates and
...re to be followed only in a very general way. The
...ctual quantity of fat, for example, that may be
...ontained in a given portion will vary with the
...uality of meat you buy or with how much care
...ou take in skimming off cooking fat. If you are on
...rigid diet, consult your physician. The analyses
...e based on the number of portions given as the
...eld for the recipe, but if the yield reads, "4 to 6
...rvings," we indicate which number of servings
..., for example) was used to determine the final
...nounts.

YIELD

- to 6-serving crust

er serving
thin crust—4 servings)
lories 316, protein 8 g,
t 8 g, sodium 539 mg,
rbohydrates 53 g,
otassium 100 mg

er serving
hick crust—4 servings)
lories 506, protein 12 g,
t 12 g, sodium 1077 mg,
rbohydrates 86 g,
otassium 141 mg

TIME

1½ hours preparation

INGREDIENTS

1 package active dry yeast
¾ cup warm water
Pinch of sugar
2 cups + 2 tablespoons all-purpose
    flour
1 teaspoon salt
1 tablespoon vegetable or olive oil

In small cup dissolve yeast in ¼ cup of the warm water mixed with sugar ①. Set aside until yeast foams.

Place 2 cups of flour in a bowl. Add salt and stir to mix. Add yeast mixture, the remaining warm water, and vegetable or olive oil. Stir to make stiff dough ②.

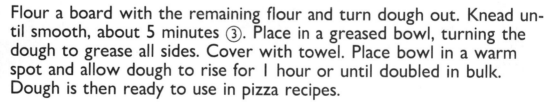

Flour a board with the remaining flour and turn dough out. Knead until smooth, about 5 minutes ③. Place in a greased bowl, turning the dough to grease all sides. Cover with towel. Place bowl in a warm spot and allow dough to rise for 1 hour or until doubled in bulk. Dough is then ready to use in pizza recipes.

VARIATION For thick-crust variation, proceed with beginning of recipe. Instead of 2 cups flour, place 3½ to 4 cups flour in bowl; add 2 teaspoons salt, 1 cup water, and 2 tablespoons oil. The thick crust dough will have to rise about 1½ hours. When preparing pizza recipe, instead of punching down, rolling out, and baking dough as for the thin crust, place thick crust in a pizza pan and cover it, then allow to rise for 30 minutes. This will give it the breadlike consistency typical of the Chicago-style deep-dish pizza.

NOTE See also recipes for Rye Pizza Crust (29) and Whole-wheat Pizza Crust (31), as well as recipe for quick Pat-a-Dough Crust (page 30).

YIELD

½ cups

Per serving (4)
calories 130, protein 3 g,
fat 8 g, sodium 549 mg,
carbohydrates 15 g,
potassium 653 mg

TIME

0 minutes preparation
1 hour cooking

INGREDIENTS

2 pounds fresh, ripe (vine-ripened)
  plum tomatoes
2 to 4 cloves garlic, peeled and
  minced
1 medium onion, chopped
2 tablespoons olive oil
¼ cup finely chopped fresh basil or
  parsley
1 teaspoon sugar (optional)
1 teaspoon salt
1 tablespoon dried oregano

Peel ①, seed (if desired) ②, and chop tomatoes. Set aside.

Sauté garlic and onion in olive oil until tender. Add tomatoes ③ and remaining ingredients except oregano. Simmer, covered, for 1 hour. Stir occasionally.

After 1 hour, add oregano and simmer uncovered until mixture is very thick. If desired, purée sauce in food processor or blender to make smooth.

NOTE See also recipe for Quick Tomato Pizza Sauce (32).

YIELD

servings

er serving

lories 518, protein 21 g,
t 27 g, sodium 1253 mg,
rbohydrates 48 g,
otassium 460 mg

TIME

¾ hours preparation
5 minutes cooking

INGREDIENTS

1 recipe Basic Pizza Crust (Recipe 1)
2 tablespoons cornmeal
1 cup Tomato Pizza Sauce (Recipes 2
    or 32)
4 ounces pepperoni, sliced thin
½ cup grated parmesan cheese
2 cups grated mozzarella cheese
½ cup diced green pepper (optional)
½ cup diced onion (optional)
½ cup sliced fresh mushrooms
    (optional)

Prepare dough for a thin-crust pizza. While it is rising, sprinkle cookie sheet with cornmeal. Preheat oven to 400 degrees. Punch dough down, then roll out on a floured board to form a 14-inch circle or a rectangle about 12 by 16 inches ①. Prick crust ②. Place crust on cookie sheet and bake in oven for 5 minutes.

Remove crust from oven and spread sauce over dough to within ½ inch of edges ③. Cut pepperoni into ½-inch pieces and sprinkle over tomato sauce. Combine cheeses and sprinkle over pepperoni. Top with green pepper, onion, and mushrooms or any combination of the 3; if desired, all 3 can be omitted.

Bake pizza for 15 minutes or until cheese melts and crust is lightly browned.

YIELD

4 to 5 servings

Per serving (4)
Calories 975, protein 37 g,
fat 42 g, sodium 1966 mg,
carbohydrates 116 g,
potassium 1142 mg

TIME

1/2 hours preparation
25 minutes cooking

INGREDIENTS

1 teaspoon honey
1 package active dry yeast
1 1/4 cups warm water
3 1/2 cups all-purpose flour
2 teaspoons salt
2 tablespoons dill weed
3 tablespoons vegetable oil

FILLING

3 1/2 cups grated mozzarella cheese
2 cups blanched and chopped fresh
broccoli (or frozen broccoli,
defrosted and well drained)

TOPPING

1 1/2 cups Tomato Pizza Sauce
(Recipes 2 or 32), heated
Freshly ground black pepper or
crushed red pepper flakes

Dissolve honey and yeast in 1/4 cup warm water and set aside until mixture bubbles.

Mix dry ingredients together, then add yeast mixture, remaining water, and oil. Turn out onto floured board and knead until dough is smooth, about 5 minutes. Place dough in an oiled bowl, turning so that top of dough is lightly covered with oil. Cover with towel and let rise in a warm place until doubled in bulk, about 1 hour.

Preheat oven to 400 degrees. Grease a 10-inch deep-dish pizza pan. Punch dough down and divide into 2 parts. Using two-thirds of the dough, form a bottom crust by pressing dough into bottom and up sides of pizza pan. Reserve remaining dough for top crust. Invert a 9-inch pie pan and grease the bottom. Pat remaining dough onto pan to make a 10-inch round, then set aside.

Mix ingredients for filling. Mound filling onto dill-crust bottom ①, then lay top crust over filling and pinch edges of crust together ②. Make a few slashes in top crust and allow steam to escape ③. Bake for 25 minutes or until top is golden. Remove pizza from oven, top with pizza sauce, and sprinkle with pepper. Bake an additional 5 minutes.

YIELD

to 6 servings

er serving (4)
alories 785, protein 36 g,
at 42 g, sodium 1703 mg,
arbohydrates 71 g,
otassium 1086 mg

TIME

hour, 50 minutes
  preparation
5 minutes cooking

INGREDIENTS

1 Whole-wheat Pizza Crust (Recipe 31)
1 cup Tomato Pizza Sauce (Recipes 2 or 32)
1 fresh tomato, sliced
1 green pepper, sliced in rings
1/3 cup sliced black olives
1 can (8 1/2 ounces) artichoke hearts, drained and quartered
1 cup broccoli flowerets
1 cup grated parmesan cheese

2 cups monterey jack cheese
1 cup alfalfa sprouts (optional)

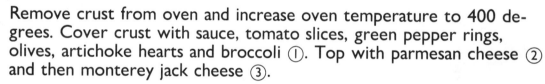

Prepare dough and when it has risen, stretch it to cover a 12-inch pizza pan. Preheat oven to 350 degrees.

Prick crust and bake for 15 minutes or until crust just begins to turn golden.

Remove crust from oven and increase oven temperature to 400 degrees. Cover crust with sauce, tomato slices, green pepper rings, olives, artichoke hearts and broccoli ①. Top with parmesan cheese ② and then monterey jack cheese ③.

Bake 15 minutes or until cheeses are melted. If desired, garnish with a ring of alfalfa sprouts arranged around perimeter of pizza.

6

YIELD

to 8 servings
er serving (6)
alories 705, protein 30 g,
at 35 g, sodium 1734 mg,
arbohydrates 66 g,
otassium 612 mg

TIME

hours preparation
hour cooking

INGREDIENTS

1 Basic Pizza Crust (Recipe 1), thick-
  crust variation
½ pound each sweet and hot Italian
  sausage, casings removed
2½ cups grated mozzarella cheese
1 cup sliced fresh mushrooms
1 cup Tomato Pizza Sauce (Recipes 2
  or 32)
½ cup grated parmesan cheese
1 egg beaten with 1 tablespoon water

Prepare dough for a thick crust, and while it is rising, continue with recipe.

Preheat oven to 350 degrees. Brown sausages together in a large skillet, breaking up meat with a fork. Drain well and set aside.

Punch dough down and roll into a rectangle 14 by 16 inches. Let rest 10 minutes, then place on cookie sheet. Sprinkle half the mozzarella cheese over half the dough leaving about ½ inch clear at the edges ①. Cover with sausage bits. Top with mushrooms, then spoon sauce over the mushrooms.

Mix remaining mozzarella cheese with parmesan cheese. Sprinkle over sauce. Fold the empty side of the dough over the filling ②. Trim off edges and press dough with fork tines to seal ③. Brush dough with egg mixture. Make 2 or 3 slashes in top of dough. Bake for 1 hour. Let sit for 10 minutes before slicing.

YIELD

servings

r serving
lories 642, protein 29 g,
: 35 g, sodium 1474 mg,
rbohydrates 53 g,
tassium 627 mg

TIME

/2 hours preparation
) minutes cooking

INGREDIENTS

1 Basic Pizza Crust (Recipe 1), thick-
   crust variation
1 cup Tomato Pizza Sauce (Recipes 2
   or 32)
1 cup peeled, seeded, and chopped
   plum tomatoes
1/2 pound each sweet and hot Italian
   sausage, casings removed
1 cup diced green pepper

2 cups sliced fresh mushrooms
3 cups grated mozzarella cheese
1 cup grated provolone cheese
1/2 cup chopped onions (optional)

Prepare dough for thick-crust pizza and while it is rising, continue with recipe. Combine pizza sauce with chopped tomatoes, and simmer, covered, for 15 minutes.

Meanwhile, brown sausages, crumbling with fork to break into small pieces ①. Drain off fat and set sausage meat aside.

Lightly grease the bottom only of a 14-inch deep-dish pizza pan. Punch dough down and roll into a 16-inch circle. Ease dough into bottom and up sides of pizza pan ②. Cover with towel and let rise in warm place for 30 minutes.

Preheat oven to 400 degrees. Bake crust for 5 minutes, then remove from oven. Spread pizza sauce over dough. Sprinkle sausage over sauce ③. Top with green pepper and mushrooms. Combine the cheeses and sprinkle over vegetables. If desired, top with onion. Bake for 30 minutes.

8

YIELD

servings

recipe analysis
ot available

TIME

hours preparation
0 minutes cooking

INGREDIENTS

1 Basic Pizza Crust (Recipe 1)
1 teaspoon dried basil
2 teaspoons dried oregano
1 tablespoon cornmeal
½ tablespoon olive oil
2 cups grated mozzarella cheese
1 cup grated monterey jack cheese
¼ cup minced scallions, mostly green
  parts
1 cup grated parmesan cheese
1 cup crumbled mild chevre (goat
  cheese)

Prepare a thin crust but knead the basil and half the oregano into the dough. While it is rising, continue with recipe.

Preheat oven to 400 degrees. Sprinkle a 10-inch deep-dish pizza pan or high-sided cake pan with cornmeal.

Punch dough down and press into bottom and sides of pan ①. Bake for 5 minutes, then remove crust from oven and brush dough with oil ②. Sprinkle on half the mozzarella cheese, then top with the monterey jack cheese. Sprinkle on scallions ③. Top with remaining mozzarella cheese, then add parmesan cheese and finally the chevre. Crumble the remaining oregano over the top and bake for 25 to 30 minutes or until cheeses are melted. Let rest 5 minutes before slicing.

YIELD

entrees or 4 appetizers
ecipe analysis
ot available

TIME

hours preparation
2 minutes cooking

INGREDIENTS

1 Basic Pizza Crust (Recipe 1)
2 tablespoons cornmeal
1 large ripe tomato
1 large green pepper
2 tablespoons olive oil
12 thin slices mozzarella cheese
2 ounces prosciutto, shredded
1 cup crumbled mild chevre (goat cheese)
2 tablespoons minced fresh basil or 2 teaspoons dried
Freshly ground black pepper

Prepare a thin crust. When it has risen, punch down dough and place on floured board. Divide into 2 equal portions, then roll each half into a 9-inch circle ①.

Preheat oven to 400 degrees. Dust a cookie sheet with cornmeal and place dough on it. Prick dough with a fork, then bake for 8 minutes.

Meanwhile, prepare vegetables. Peel, core, and seed tomato, then dice and set aside. Core and thinly slice the pepper. Heat the oil in a medium skillet. Add green pepper strips and sauté 5 minutes. Set aside.

Remove dough from oven. Arrange mozzarella cheese over both crusts to cover ②. Divide tomato pieces between pizzas. Arrange pepper strips over tomatoes. Sprinkle with prosciutto, then top with chevre. Sprinkle with basil and a generous amount of pepper. Drizzle the remaining oil from sautéing the peppers over the pizzas ③. Bake about 12 minutes or until edges of crusts are golden.

YIELD

to 7 servings

er serving (5)
lories 800, protein 44 g,
t 50 g, sodium 2202 mg,
rbohydrates 44 g,
tassium 645 mg

TIME

0 minutes preparation
hour cooking

INGREDIENTS

2 packages (10 ounces each) chopped
 spinach, defrosted and squeezed
 dry
½ cup sliced scallions, both green and
 white parts
¾ cup crumbled ricotta
1½ cups crumbled feta cheese
1 cup grated mozzarella cheese
4 tablespoons grated parmesan cheese

¼ cup minced fresh parsley
3 eggs, beaten
1 teaspoon salt
Several grindings of black pepper
8 ounces phyllo dough
2 tablespoons butter, melted

Preheat oven to 350 degrees. Grease inside of a 10-inch deep-dish pizza pan.

In a large bowl, combine spinach, scallions, cheeses, parsley, eggs, salt, and pepper. Cover bottom and sides of pan with phyllo dough ①, folding edges over so that ¼ inch extends above rim of the pan. Sprinkle dough on bottom of the pan with melted butter ②. Fill with spinach mixture, then use any remaining phyllo dough to make decorations on top of spinach ③. Bake 50 minutes.

Increase oven temperature to 450 degrees and bake pizza an additional 10 minutes or until dough turns golden.

YIELD

servings
er serving
lories 709, protein 36 g,
t 34 g, sodium 1095 mg,
rbohydrates 67 g,
tassium 764 mg

TIME

hours preparation
0 minutes cooking

INGREDIENTS

I Basic Pizza Crust (Recipe I)
½ cup cornmeal
I pound ground beef
I can (16 to 20 ounces) tomatoes, drained
2 tablespoons tomato paste
2 teaspoons chili powder
I teaspoon ground cumin
Salt and black pepper
I cup chopped onion
I can (15 ounces) refried beans
¼ cup chopped fresh cilantro (optional)
1½ teaspoons crushed red chili peppers
2 cups grated monterey jack cheese
I soft medium avocado
I clove garlic, peeled and mashed
Dash of hot pepper sauce
I tablespoon lemon juice
¼ cup peeled, seeded, and chopped fresh plum tomato

Prepare a thin crust, kneading the cornmeal into the dough. Set aside to rise.

Preheat oven to 400 degrees. Prepare the filling. Brown the beef in a large skillet, then pour off all the fat. Break up the tomatoes and seed them if desired. Add tomatoes to meat along with tomato paste, chili powder, cumin, I teaspoon salt, and ¼ teaspoon pepper. Stir in half the onions and simmer 10 minutes.

To assemble, punch dough down. Press dough into bottom and up sides of a 14-inch deep-dish pizza pan. Bake for 5 minutes.

Remove crust from oven and spread with refried beans ①. Gently spread meat sauce over beans ②. Sprinkle with cilantro if desired. Season liberally with pepper. Sprinkle with chili peppers, then spread cheese over this. Top with remaining onions. Bake for 20 minutes or until cheese has melted and crust is light brown.

Meanwhile, prepare guacamole topping. In a medium bowl, mash avocado with the back of a fork ③. Add garlic, hot pepper sauce, salt and pepper to taste, lemon juice, and tomato. Stir gently and set aside until pizza is ready. When serving, top each pizza slice with a dollop of guacamole.

YIELD

to 6 servings

er serving (4)
lories 518, protein 17 g,
t 18 g, sodium 2212 mg,
rbohydrates 72 g,
tassium 1018 mg

TIME

/2 hours preparation
5 minutes cooking

INGREDIENTS

1 Basic Pizza Crust (Recipe 1)
1 tablespoon olive oil
1 cup canned tomatoes, broken into
   pieces
1 ½ cups tomato purée
¼ cup tomato paste
1 large or 2 small cloves garlic,
   peeled
½ teaspoon salt

1 ½ teaspoons dried basil
2 tablespoons cornmeal
2 cans (2 ounces each) anchovy fillets,
   drained
20 dark salty olives, pitted

Prepare dough and while it is rising, continue with recipe.

Heat oil in a skillet. Add tomatoes and simmer over medium heat for 5 to 10 minutes or until liquid is thick and syrupy. Add tomato purée and tomato paste ①. Mash garlic with salt until a paste ② and add to tomato mixture. Stir in basil. Cover; simmer 20 minutes.

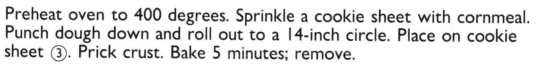

Preheat oven to 400 degrees. Sprinkle a cookie sheet with cornmeal. Punch dough down and roll out to a 14-inch circle. Place on cookie sheet ③. Prick crust. Bake 5 minutes; remove.

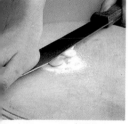

Spread crust with tomato mixture, then arrange 3 rows of anchovy fillets in vertical strips over the tomato mixture. Make 4 crosswise rows, and place 1 olive in each square, about 20 in all. Bake for 15 minutes.

YIELD

to 5 servings

er serving (4)
lories 939, protein 40 g,
t 39 g, sodium 1046 mg,
rbohydrates 108 g,
tassium 896 mg

TIME

/2 hours preparation
0 minutes cooking

INGREDIENTS

1 teaspoon honey
1 1/4 cups warm water
1 package active dry yeast
2 1/2 cups all-purpose flour
1 cup whole-wheat flour
1 teaspoon salt
3 tablespoons olive oil

FILLING

1 pound ground beef
1 onion, chopped
1 teaspoon ground cloves

2 teaspoons ground cumin
Freshly ground black pepper to taste
1/4 cup tomato paste
1 cup water
1/3 cup raisins
1/3 cup pinenuts (pignoli) or walnuts
1/3 cup sliced pimiento-stuffed green
olives

GLAZE

1 egg white
1 tablespoon water

Dissolve honey in 1/4 cup warm water and then add the yeast. Set aside until yeast foams.

Mix flours and salt, then add yeast mixture, remaining water, and oil. Turn out onto a floured board and knead until dough is smooth, about 5 minutes. Place dough in an oiled bowl, turning dough so that top of dough is lightly covered with oil. Cover with towel and let rise in a warm place until doubled in bulk, about 1 hour.

Brown meat in a skillet with the onion. Spoon off grease ①, then add cloves, cumin, pepper, tomato paste, water, and raisins. Simmer until water boils off and mixture is almost dry. Stir in nuts and olives and set aside.

Grease a 10-inch deep-dish pizza pan or baking dish. When dough has risen, punch down and divide into 2 parts. Using two-thirds of the dough, form a bottom crust by pressing into bottom and up sides of pan ②. To shape top crust, invert a 9-inch pie pan, grease the bottom, and pat dough onto pan to make a 10-inch round. Set aside.

Preheat oven to 400 degrees. Mound the filling into the dough-lined pan, allowing 1 inch of dough around the outside edge to remain uncovered. Top with the remaining dough and pinch the edges shut. Make a few slashes in top to allow steam to escape.

Mix egg white and water together for the glaze. Brush onto pastry top ③ and bake 30 minutes or until pizza is golden.

YIELD

to 6 servings

r serving (4)
lories 950, protein 43 g,
t 56 g, sodium 2312 mg,
rbohydrates 76 g,
tassium 1129 mg

TIME

hour, 40 minutes
preparation
) minutes cooking

INGREDIENTS

1 Whole-wheat Crust (Recipe 32)
¼ cup vegetable oil
1 medium onion, sliced thin
2 cloves garlic, peeled and minced
1 tablespoon minced gingerroot
3 small green chilies, finely chopped
½ to ¾ pound very lean ground beef
1 can (16 ounces) tomatoes, chopped and
    drained, with juice reserved
3 tablespoons tomato paste
2 teaspoons salt
⅛ teaspoon each ground cinnamon and
    cloves

¼ teaspoon ground cardamon
1½ teaspoons ground cumin
1 teaspoon paprika
¼ teaspoon freshly ground black pepper

TOPPINGS

1 cup fresh or frozen peas
1 small cauliflower, about 8 ounces
⅛ teaspoon turmeric
1 small plum tomato, thinly sliced
2 cups grated muenster cheese
2 tablespoons chopped fresh coriander
1 lemon, cut in wedges

Prepare dough and while it is rising, continue with recipe. In a large, heavy saucepan, heat oil. Add onion and fry over medium heat, stirring constantly, until onion turns a rich cara-mel brown. (As onion begins to brown, lower or shut off heat and continue stirring. Do not allow to burn.) When onion has browned, add garlic, ginger, chili peppers, and ground beef ①, stirring over medium heat until beef is browned and broken into small pieces. Add the drained tomatoes, tomato paste, salt, spices, black pepper and up to 1 cup of reserved tomato juice. Stir to combine. Simmer, covered, over low heat for 30 minutes, stirring occasionally so that flavors have a chance to blend. If the mixture (keema) starts to stick to bottom of saucepan, add a couple of tablespoons of water. Do not add too much water; the mixture should be thick.

Cook peas in a small amount of water and drain. Separate cauliflower into small flower-ets ②. Place in pan with a small amount of water to which turmeric has been added. Bring to a boil, lower heat, and simmer just until cauliflower is tender-crisp. Drain.

Preheat oven to 400 degrees. Grease a 12-inch pizza pan with oil. Punch dough down and stretch to cover pizza pan. Prick the crust and bake for 8 minutes. Brush pizza crust lightly with oil, then spread keema evenly over top of dough. Arrange cauliflower and tomato slices decoratively over top ③. Sprinkle peas evenly over top, then sprinkle cheese on top of pizza. Let rest 10 minutes.

Bake 20 to 25 minutes at 400 degrees or until cheese is golden. Remove from oven and sprinkle fresh coriander over top. Let pizza sit 5 minutes before serving. Serve with lemon wedges and allow guests to sprinkle individual portions with fresh lemon juice to taste.

YIELD

to 6 servings

er serving
, with shrimp)
lories 795, protein 32 g,
t 40 g, sodium 2416 mg,
rbohydrates 80 g,
tassium 1418 mg

TIME

hours preparation
minutes cooking

INGREDIENTS

1 Rye Pizza Crust (Recipe 29)
1 clove garlic, peeled and minced
1 green pepper, seeded and chopped
2 tablespoons olive oil
1 can (16 ounces) tomatoes, drained
  and chopped
1 cup Tomato Pizza Sauce (Recipes 2
  or 32)
2 teaspoons salt
4 tablespoons butter
1 pound seafood of choice, cut into
  bite-sized pieces

Prepare dough and while it is rising, continue with recipe.

Preheat oven to 450 degrees. Sauté garlic and green pepper in olive oil until limp. Add tomatoes, pizza sauce, and salt; cover and simmer 15 minutes.

Grease a 12-inch pizza pan with oil. Punch dough down and stretch to cover pan. Prick crust ① and bake for 8 minutes or until crust just begins to turn golden around the edges. Remove from oven. Reduce heat to 350 degrees.

Melt butter in saucepan and sauté seafood until cooked, about 3 minutes. Remove from butter with slotted spoon and combine with tomato mixture ②. Pour seafood mixture into partially baked pizza crust ③ and bake for 30 minutes or until pizza is heated through.

YIELD

to 6 servings

er serving (4)
lories 993, protein 41 g,
t 54 g, sodium 2997 mg,
rbohydrates 89 g,
tassium 971 mg

TIME

hours preparation
) minutes cooking

INGREDIENTS

1 Rye Pizza Crust (Recipe 29)
6 cups thinly sliced yellow onions
4 tablespoons olive oil
4 tablespoons beef bouillon granules
    dissolved in 4 tablespoons hot
    water
2 tablespoons caraway seeds
2 cups grated parmesan cheese
2 cups grated mozzarella cheese

Prepare dough and while it is rising, continue with recipe.

Sauté onions in oil until soft. Add bouillon and water mixture ① and cook until all liquid is boiled off. Stir often.

Preheat oven to 450 degrees. Grease a 12-inch pizza pan with oil ②.

Punch dough down and stretch it to cover the pan. Prick crust and bake for 8 minutes or until crust just begins to brown. Remove, and reduce oven temperature to 350 degrees.

Mound onions onto baked pizza crust ③. Sprinkle with caraway seeds and top with parmesan and then mozzarella cheese. Bake pizza for 30 minutes or until cheeses are melted.

IELD

to 6 servings

er serving (4)
alories 798, protein 35 g,
t 48 g, sodium 1426 mg,
arbohydrates 62 g,
otassium 732 mg

IME

hour, 45 minutes
preparation
0 minutes cooking

INGREDIENTS

1 Whole-wheat Pizza Crust (Recipe
  31)
½ cup pesto sauce
1½ cups thinly sliced fresh
  mushrooms
1½ cups grated parmesan cheese
1½ cups grated mozzarella cheese
3 scallions, sliced both white and
  green parts

Prepare dough and allow to rise.

Preheat oven to 400 degrees. Punch dough down and stretch to fit a 12-inch pizza pan. Prick crust ① and bake for 10 minutes or until crust just begins to turn golden. Reduce oven temperature to 350 degrees.

Spread crust with pesto sauce ②. Arrange mushrooms on top, leaving a narrow ring of pesto as a border. Top with parmesan and then mozzarella cheese. Sprinkle with scallions ③. Bake for 30 minutes or until cheese is melted.

NOTE Pesto sauce is available in many gourmet food stores. In addition, many cookbooks have recipes for making this basil sauce.

YIELD

loaf

Per serving (12)
Calories 266, protein 8 g,
fat 10 g, sodium 428 mg,
carbohydrates 35 g,
potassium 176 mg

TIME

hours, 40 minutes
   preparation
8 minutes cooking

INGREDIENTS

1 teaspoon honey
¼ cup warm water
1 package active dry yeast
3½ cups all-purpose flour
1 teaspoon salt
2 tablespoons dried oregano
1 tablespoon sugar
1 cup sliced scallions, both white and
   green parts
1 cup sliced pepperoni

1 cup milk
2 tablespoons olive oil
¼ cup Tomato Pizza Sauce (Recipes
   2 or 32), heated
⅓ cup grated mozzarella cheese

Dissolve honey in warm water. Add yeast and set aside until mixture bubbles.

Mix flour, salt, oregano, sugar, scallions, and pepperoni together. Add milk, yeast mixture, and olive oil. Blend, then turn out onto a floured board and knead until dough is smooth ①, about 8 minutes. Place dough in an oiled bowl, turning it so that the top of the dough is lightly covered with oil ②. Cover with a towel and let rise in a warm place until doubled in bulk, about 1 hour.

Punch dough down. Knead for 1 minute, then transfer to an oiled 9-by-5-by-3-inch loaf pan. Cover with a towel and let rise again in warm place until doubled in bulk, about 1 hour.

Preheat oven to 375 degrees. Bake bread for 35 minutes or until bread sounds hollow when tapped. Brush loaf with pizza sauce ③ and sprinkle cheese in a strip down center of bread. Return loaf to oven and bake until cheese melts, about 3 minutes.

YIELD

to 8 servings

er serving (6)
lories 889, protein 52 g,
t 59 g, sodium 2138 mg,
rbohydrates 38 g,
tassium 1173 mg

TIME

0 minutes preparation
5 minutes cooking

INGREDIENTS

1 pound hot or sweet Italian sausage,
   casings removed
1 pound ground beef
2 cloves garlic, peeled and minced
1 onion, chopped
1 can (16 ounces) stewed tomatoes
1 can (10¾ ounces) tomato purée
1 can (6 ounces) tomato paste
¾ cup water

1 teaspoon salt
1 tablespoon dried oregano
1 tablespoon fennel seeds
1 teaspoon to 1 tablespoon crushed
   red pepper
Freshly ground black pepper to taste
1 package (1 pound) noodles, cooked
4 cups grated cheddar cheese
2 cups grated mozzarella cheese

Preheat oven to 350 degrees. Brown sausage and beef in large saucepan. Pour off grease, then add garlic, onion, tomatoes with juice, tomato purée, tomato paste, water, and seasonings ①. Simmer, covered, for 15 minutes.

Grease a 14-inch deep-dish pizza pan with oil. Layer in the ingredients, beginning with all the cooked noodles. Top noodles with meat mixture ②, then sprinkle with cheddar and mozzarella cheese ③. Bake for 25 minutes or until ingredients are heated through and cheeses have melted.

YIELD

entrees, 8 appetizers

er serving (4)

alories 931, protein 38 g,
at 54 g, sodium 2860 mg,
arbohydrates 74 g,
otassium 666 mg

TIME

0 minutes preparation
0 minutes cooking

INGREDIENTS

I loaf French bread (16 inches long,
   4 inches wide)
2¼ 4 tablespoons olive oil
¾ cup Tomato Pizza Sauce (Recipes
   2 or 32)
I cup chopped salami or summer
   sausage (quarter a sausage, then
   cut chunks ½ inch thick)
I cup pimiento-stuffed green olives
I cup grated parmesan cheese
I½ cups grated mozzarella cheese
I green pepper, cut in strips

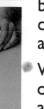

Preheat broiler. Cut top quarter from bread ①. Remove all but ½-inch layer of bread from inside crust ②. (Leftover bread top and insides can be used to make bread crumbs.) Brush the inside of the loaf with 2 tablespoons olive oil ③ and place under broiler until edges turn golden. Watch carefully; this only takes a minute.

Reduce the oven temperature to 350 degrees. Spread the inside of the bread with sauce. Top with salami, olives, parmesan, and mozzarella cheese. Bake for 30 minutes or until ingredients are heated through and cheeses are melted.

While bread is baking, sauté the green pepper strips in the remaining olive oil. Drain, then top baked pizza bread with sautéed peppers. Slice and serve.

YIELD

rolls

er serving
alories 267, protein 7 g,
t 13 g, sodium 696 mg,
rbohydrates 30 g,
otassium 331 mg

IME

hours preparation
0 minutes cooking

INGREDIENTS

1 Basic Pizza Crust (Recipe 1)
4 tablespoons olive oil
1 large clove garlic, peeled and
  minced
1 cup chopped onion
1½ cups tomato purée
4 tablespoons tomato paste
1 teaspoon dried oregano
½ teaspoon salt
Generous dash of black pepper
1 tablespoon minced fresh parsley
⅔ cup grated parmesan cheese

Prepare dough and while it is rising, continue with recipe. Heat oil in a medium skillet. Add garlic and onion and sauté for 10 minutes, or until onion is transparent. Stir in tomato purée, tomato paste, oregano, salt, pepper, and parsley. Simmer 5 minutes, then cool to room temperature.

Punch dough down. Roll out on a floured board to a 10 by 14-inch rectangle. Spread with sauce, leaving 1 inch uncoated around the edge ①.

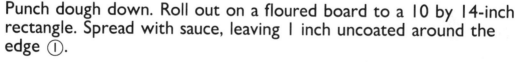

Roll up 10-inch side to create a 14-inch-long roll ②. Press edges to seal. If necessary wet edges with a little water to seal firmly. With a sharp knife, cut roll into 9 even slices, each about 1½ inches wide.

Place rolls cut side up on a greased cookie sheet ③. Sprinkle about 1 tablespoon of parmesan cheese over each roll. Place in warm area, cover with towel, and let rise 30 minutes.

Preheat oven to 375 degrees. Bake rolls for 25 to 30 minutes, or until dough has browned and cheese has melted.

YIELD

to 8 servings

Per serving (6)
Calories 735, protein 30 g,
fat 44 g, sodium 2162 mg,
carbohydrates 56 g,
potassium 1177 mg

TIME

¾ hours preparation
0 minutes cooking

INGREDIENTS

1 Basic Pizza Crust (Recipe 1)
6 tablespoons olive oil
4 cups sliced mushrooms
1 cup diced green pepper
1 clove garlic, peeled and minced
1 cup minced onion
1 pound sweet Italian sausage, casings
   removed
1 can (28 ounces) tomato purée

2 tablespoons tomato paste
1½ teaspoons dried oregano
1½ teaspoons crushed fennel seeds
1 teaspoon salt
Black pepper to taste
1 tablespoon minced fresh parsley
2 cups diced mozzarella cheese
1 cup grated parmesan cheese
1 egg, beaten

Prepare pizza dough and while it is rising, continue with recipe.

Preheat oven to 350 degrees. Heat 4 tablespoons oil in a skillet. Add mushrooms and green pepper and sauté for 10 minutes over low heat. Remove mushrooms and pepper and add remaining oil to skillet. Add garlic and onion and sauté 5 minutes. Then add sausage and brown, breaking up with a fork. Pour off all the fat and return mushrooms and peppers to skillet.

Stir in tomato purée, tomato paste, oregano, fennel seeds, salt, pepper, and parsley. Simmer 10 minutes. Then spoon tomato mixture into a shallow baking pan, about 3 inches high, 13 inches long, and 8½ inches at its widest ①. Toss cheeses together and sprinkle over tomato mixture.

Punch dough down on a floured board. Roll out to an oval about 1½ inches larger than baking pan ②. Place over pan, pressing the edges of dough to dish to seal ③. Brush dough with beaten egg, then make 2 slashes at top of dough. Place on top of cookie sheet and bake for 30 minutes.

PIZZA QUICHE

YIELD

0 appetizers

er serving
lories 626, protein 32 g,
t 44 g, sodium 1442 mg,
rbohydrates 25 g,
tassium 308 mg

TIME

5 minutes preparation
5 minutes cooking

INGREDIENTS

1 Pat-a-Dough Crust (Recipe 30)
2½ cups grated sharp cheddar cheese
1½ cups grated mozzarella cheese
1 cup grated swiss cheese
4 eggs
1 cup diced pepperoni
1 cup red salsa, preferably hot

Preheat oven to 400 degrees. Pat dough into bottom and up the sides of a 10-inch deep-dish pizza pan or pie plate with high sides ①. Bake for 5 minutes. Remove from oven and reduce temperature to 350 degrees.

Combine cheeses. Sprinkle half the cheese mixture over crust ②. Beat together eggs, pepperoni, and salsa, then pour the egg mixture over the cheese ③. Top with remaining cheese mixture.

Bake quiche for 45 minutes or until set. Cut into small wedges to serve. This pizza will be easier to cut if allowed to stand for 10 minutes first.

NOTE Salsa is available in ethnic food sections of most supermarkets. If not available, substitute chili sauce.

YIELD

servings

er serving
alories 613, protein 31 g,
t 39 g, sodium 992 mg,
rbohydrates 34 g,
otassium 566 mg

TIME

bout 6 hours preparation
bout 1 hour cooking

INGREDIENTS

12 thin slices white sandwich bread
1 can (28 ounces) whole peeled
   tomatoes
1 tablespoon olive oil
Salt and black pepper
1 tablespoon minced fresh basil or 1
   teaspoon dried
2 ounces pepperoni, sliced thin and
   diced

2 cups grated swiss cheese
2 cups grated mozzarella cheese
4 eggs
1½ cups half-and-half

Butter a shallow 10-inch casserole or pizza pan. Cut bread slices in half; form 24 triangles. Arrange 8 triangles in the bottom of the pan in a pinwheel design ①. Set aside.

Drain tomatoes. Heat oil in a heavy-bottomed skillet, then add tomatoes. Break up into bits and cook over medium heat until liquid has almost evaporated and mixture thickens, about 20 minutes. Stir in salt and pepper to taste and basil. Simmer 5 minutes.

Arrange pepperoni pieces over bread. Combine cheeses, then sprinkle half over the pepperoni. Cover with tomato sauce ②.

Cover sauce with 8 more triangles. Top with remaining cheese and cover with remaining bread triangles. Beat together eggs and half-and-half, then pour carefully over bread ③. Cover with plastic wrap and refrigerate several hours or overnight.

Remove dish from refrigerator about 30 minutes before baking. Preheat oven to 350 degrees. Bake casserole for 1 hour or until cheese has melted and dish is puffy. Let stand 5 minutes before slicing.

YIELD

bout 100 appetizers

er appetizer
lories 29, protein 2 g,
t 2 g, sodium 82 mg,
rbohydrates 2 g,
tassium 32 mg

TIME

0 minutes preparation
0 minutes cooking

INGREDIENTS

Vegetable oil for deep frying
8 ounces egg-roll wrappers, cut in
  bite-sized rounds (about 9 per
  egg-roll wrapper)
3 tablespoons soy sauce
1 teaspoon salt
1/2 teaspoon black pepper
2 teaspoons 5-spice powder (or any
  combination of ground cloves,
  cinnamon, fennel seed, Sichuan
  peppercorns, and/or star anise)
1 teaspoon sugar

2 teaspoons cornstarch
8 ounces ground pork or shredded
  cooked roast beef
8 ounces bean sprouts, chopped
1 can (8 ounces) waterchestnuts,
  drained and chopped
1 can (4 ounces) bamboo shoots,
  drained and chopped
4 scallions, sliced both white and
  green parts
4 ounces tiny shrimp, cooked
1 1/2 cups grated mozzarella cheese

Heat oil to 375 degrees. Then deep-fry the egg roll rounds until light golden ①. Drain on paper towels and set aside.

Combine soy sauce, salt, black pepper, 5-spice powder, sugar, and cornstarch in a bowl and set aside.

Preheat oven to 350 degrees. In a wok or large skillet, stir-fry the pork, breaking it up into small pieces, until pork is no longer pink. Pour off grease and add bean sprouts, waterchestnuts, bamboo shoots, scallions, and shrimp. Stir-fry for a minute until heated through, then add soy sauce mixture. Combine and cook until thickened.

Pile the filling onto the egg-roll rounds ②, sprinkle with cheese ③, and bake for 5 minutes or until heated through. Serve hot.

YIELD

0 rolls

er roll

lories 182, protein 6 g,
t 12 g, sodium 389 mg,
rbohydrates 13 g,
tassium 153 mg

TIME

/2 hours preparation
0 minutes cooking

INGREDIENTS

2½ tablespoons olive oil
1 large clove garlic, peeled and
  minced
¾ cup seeded and diced green pepper
1 pound sweet Italian sausage, casings
  removed
14 ounces (½ a 28-ounce can)
  crushed, peeled tomatoes
¼ cup tomato paste
½ teaspoon dried oregano

½ teaspoon salt
Pinch of sugar
⅛ teaspoon dried rosemary
Black pepper to taste
1½ cups diced mozzarella cheese
  (in ¼-inch dice)
1 package (16 ounces) egg-roll
  wrappers
1 egg, beaten
2 cups vegetable oil

Heat 2 tablespoons olive oil in a heavy-bottomed skillet. Add garlic and green pepper and sauté over medium heat for 5 minutes. Add sausage and crumble the meat with a spoon. Brown thoroughly, then drain off the fat. Add the crushed tomatoes and tomato paste, and simmer 10 minutes. Add seasonings and simmer 10 more minutes. Stir in the remaining olive oil. Allow to cool. When ready to assemble the rolls, stir in the cheese.

Fill one wrapper at a time. Place ⅓ cup of filling one-third the way up from one corner of the skin ①. Roll egg-roll wrapper and filling up almost to the opposite end ②. Brush egg on both open ends and fold into center of egg roll. Brush beaten egg on opposite end to seal; finish rolling ③. Set aside and repeat with remaining egg rolls.

Heat oil in a heavy-bottomed skillet. Fry egg-rolls 4 at a time over medium heat for 2 to 3 minutes per side, or until golden. Remove and drain on paper towels. Repeat with remaining egg-rolls.

APPLE PIZZA PIE

YIELD

2 to 16 servings

per serving (12)
calories 539, protein 6 g,
fat 24 g, sodium 351 mg,
carbohydrates 77 g,
potassium 274 mg

TIME

hour preparation
hour cooking

INGREDIENTS

Double recipe Pat-a-dough Crust
   (Recipe 30)
1 cup apple butter
2 tablespoons bourbon
6 large baking apples, peeled, cored,
   and thinly sliced
½ cup light or dark raisins
¾ cup chopped walnuts
1 cup sugar
2 to 3 teaspoons ground cinnamon
¾ cup all-purpose flour
½ cup butter, cut into small pieces

Preheat oven to 400 degrees. Prepare dough and press into bottom and slightly up sides of a 14-inch deep-dish pizza pan. Bake for 5 minutes. Remove from oven and reduce oven temperature to 350 degrees.

Mix together apple butter and bourbon. Gently spread over bottom of pie crust to make a very thin coating ①. Toss together apples, raisins, and nuts. Sprinkle apple mixture over crust ②.

Combine half the sugar with the cinnamon. Sprinkle over apple slices. Mix together flour and remaining sugar, then cut in butter until mixture is crumbly. Sprinkle over sugar mixture ③. Bake for 50 to 60 minutes or until crust is light brown. Serve warm.

YIELD

2 servings

Per serving

Calories 588, protein 9 g,
fat 31 g, sodium 334 mg,
carbohydrates 70 g,
potassium 179 mg

TIME

0 minutes preparation
1/2 hours cooking

INGREDIENTS

- 1 Pat-a-dough Crust (Recipe 30)
- 2 1/4 cups sugar
- 1 cup water
- 1/2 teaspoon ground ginger
- 1 pint cherry tomatoes, stems removed
- 24 ounces cream cheese, at room temperature
- 4 eggs
- 1/2 cup heavy cream
- 1/2 teaspoon vanilla extract
- 1 jar (10 ounces) tomato preserves
- 2 tablespoons orange-flavored liqueur or orange juice

Preheat oven to 400 degrees. Prepare pat-a-dough, then press into bottom and sides of 10-inch deep-dish pizza pan. Bake for 8 minutes. Remove from oven and set aside. Reduce oven temperature to 300 degrees.

Combine 1 cup of sugar with water in a saucepan. Stir over medium heat to dissolve sugar, then stir in ginger. Halve the tomatoes and stir in. Simmer about 10 minutes, until tomatoes become tender and skins loosen. Remove skins and drain off all but 2 tablespoons of liquid from the pan. Set aside.

Place cream cheese in the bowl of an electric mixer. Add the remaining sugar and beat until creamy, occasionally scraping down sides of bowl. Add eggs, 1 at a time, then add cream and vanilla. Blend well.

Heat half the jar of tomato preserves with 1 tablespoon of orange-flavored liqueur. Spread over the bottom of the crust ①, then pour in filling. Place pan inside a larger pan with enough hot water to come up 1 inch on the outside of the pan ②. Place pizza in oven for 1 hour.

While pizza is baking, combine reserved tomatoes in saucepan with remaining tomato preserves and remaining orange-flavored liqueur. Simmer 5 minutes to thicken slightly. Set aside to cool.

Remove pizza from oven and spread tomato mixture over it ③. Return to water bath in oven for an additional 30 minutes. Remove the pizza from the oven in its water bath and allow to cool to room temperature. Remove and refrigerate 4 hours before serving.

RYE PIZZA CRUST

YIELD

12- to 14-inch thin crust

Per serving (4)
calories 380, protein 8 g,
fat 11 g, sodium 549 mg,
carbohydrates 62 g,
potassium 427 mg

TIME

1 hour, 20 minutes
preparation

INGREDIENTS

1 package active dry yeast
1 teaspoon honey
3/4 cup warm water
1 cup all-purpose flour
1 1/3 cups medium rye flour
1 teaspoon salt
2 tablespoons dark molasses
2 tablespoons vegetable or olive oil

Dissolve yeast and honey in 1/4 cup warm water and set aside until yeast foams.

Place both flours in a large bowl. Add yeast mixture, salt, molasses, oi and 1/2 cup water and stir to combine. Turn dough out into a floured board and knead until dough is smooth, about 5 minutes. Place dough in an oiled bowl, turning so that top of dough is lightly covered with oil. Cover with towel and let rise in warm place until doubled in bulk, about 1 hour.

PAT-A-DOUGH CRUST

YIELD

10-inch crust

Per serving (4)
calories 328, protein 5 g,
fat 17 g, sodium 408 mg,
carbohydrates 39 g,
potassium 58 mg

TIME

15 minutes preparation

INGREDIENTS

1 1/2 cups all-purpose flour
3/4 teaspoon salt
2 teaspoons sugar
4 1/2 tablespoons vegetable oil
2 tablespoons milk

Into a bowl or 10-inch deep-dish pizza pan, sift together flour, salt, an sugar. Beat together oil and milk and pour into the flour mixture. Mix with fingers until dough is dampened and crumbly. (Dough will never come together like a conventional pastry dough.) Press dough into bottom and sides of pizza pan. Crust is ready to be used in pizza recipe.

WHOLE-WHEAT PIZZA CRUST

YIELD

12- to 14-inch thin crust

Per serving (4)
Calories 335, protein 8 g,
fat 12 g, sodium 540 mg,
carbohydrates 51 g,
potassium 181 mg

TIME

1 hour, 20 minutes
preparation

INGREDIENTS

1 package active dry yeast
1 teaspoon honey
3/4 cup warm water
1 cup all-purpose flour
1 cup whole-wheat flour
1 teaspoon salt
2 tablespoons olive oil

Dissolve yeast and honey in 1/4 cup warm water and set aside until yeast foams.

Place both flours in a large bowl. Add yeast mixture, salt, olive oil, and remaining water. Stir to combine.

Turn dough out onto a floured board and knead until smooth, about 5 minutes. Place dough in an oiled bowl, turning so that top of dough is lightly covered with oil. Cover with towel. Let rise in warm place until doubled in bulk, about 1 hour.

QUICK TOMATO PIZZA SAUCE

YIELD

1 cup

Per serving (4)
Calories 57, protein 2 g,
1 g, sodium 692 mg,
carbohydrates 11 g,
potassium 492 mg

TIME

minutes preparation
minutes cooking

INGREDIENTS

1 to 2 cloves garlic, peeled and
   minced
1 teaspoon olive oil
1 can (8 to 10 ounces) tomato purée
   or tomato sauce
1/4 cup tomato paste
1/2 teaspoon salt
1 teaspoon dried basil
2 teaspoons dried oregano
Several grindings of black pepper

Over low heat, sauté garlic in olive oil until garlic is softened but not brown. Add remaining ingredients and stir to combine. Simmer, covered, over very low heat for 15 minutes.

INDEX